One Second After You Die

FIRST PRINTING

Billy Crone

Cover Design:
Get A Life Media

To my brother, Jim.

As I look back on this life,
I am amazed and humbled at the manifold wisdom of God.
What I mean is this.
Of all the people that the Lord would ordain to overshadow me,
via an only older brother,
it was and is you.

Thank you for the sharing of your time,
your patience, your wisdom, and very life in me.
It has proven to be an investment in God's hands,
to help mold me into a responsible man.

At times, you have been more than a brother to me,
but a father figure as well, when I needed it most.
Thank you, Jim.
I love you.

Contents

Preface

When I was a "brand new" Christian I was busy doing what I figured *all* Christians should do and that is, witnessing. I was learning new and exciting information each day as I had enrolled in Bible College eight weeks after being saved. One day, I was engaged in a conversation with my brother Jim concerning the Book of Genesis and the conditions of the Garden of Eden prior to the fall of man. As we continued to talk, I was challenged with the classical response of, "How do I know it's true?" This hit me like a ton of bricks. I knew the Bible was God's Word but this was the first time that I was asked for "proof." I stumbled through the rest of the conversation and left shortly thereafter. That night I prayed a prayer that changed the course of this life. I cried out, "God, I don't want to be a 'copycat Christian.' I do not want to merely repeat or 'copy' what I learn about the Scriptures from my instructors, even though I do not doubt their integrity, but I want to know for myself, *why I believe what I believe.*" From then on, I began to not only study the truth of God's Word but to understand it from all angles, skeptic and non-skeptic alike. This has proven to be a powerful force in enabling God to use this life right on up to today in "giving a reason for the hope that lies within me."

Now, even though this is clearly a mandate for all believers to fulfill, I have noticed that over the years, although there are volumes of apologetic books out there to equip the Christian to give a proper defense and aid them in effective witnessing, many people still will not pick them up. Some might buy one or two in their lifetime but they seem have a hard time in reading them due to the "technical" language that is by necessity contained within. The constant complaint seems to be "It's too hard to understand. It's too boring." Therefore, the purpose of this book is not to merely hand you yet another apologetic book on popular questions raised by the skeptic concerning the Bible, but one that is *easy* to understand and follow, and believe it or not, actually *fun* to read! My desire is that you will not only finish this book, but that you would join me in a passionate pursuit of God's truth and share it with every soul that the Lord would put in your path. One last piece of advice. When you are through reading this book then will you please READ YOUR BIBLE? I mean that in the nicest possible way. Enjoy, and I'm looking forward to seeing you someday!

Billy Crone
Las Vegas, Nevada
2018

Chapter One

Is There Life After Death?

"One day this Amish boy and his father were visiting a mall and they were amazed by almost everything they saw, especially the two shiny, silver walls that could move apart and then slide back together again.

The boy asked his Father, 'What is this, Father?'

And the Father said, (never having seen an elevator before), 'Son, I have no idea. I've never seen anything like this in my life,'

So as the boy and his father were watching with amazement, a rather heavy, not too attractive, older lady walked up to the moving walls and pressed a button.

And sure enough, the walls opened, and the lady walked right in-between them and entered a small room, and as the walls closed again, the boy and his father were watching the small circular numbers above, the doors light up.

They continued to watch until it reached the last number and then the numbers began to light in the reverse order. Finally, the walls opened up again, but this time, a young beautiful woman stepped out.

The Father leaned over to his son and said, 'Son, go get your Mother.'"

Okay, granted maybe elevators can't transform your wife, but if you stop and think about it properly, *they can actually transform your life*. How? Because it works like this. You see, an elevator has two destinations. Either up or down. And the Bible weaves the same tale for every one of us. Each one of us here is currently headed for eternal bliss in heaven, or eternal torment in hell. Yet, in our skeptical world today, many people not only scoff at the Bible but they even scoff at the claims of Jesus, who said in the Bible, that He's the only One and the Only Way to not just get us to heaven, but to save us from hell! And you can scoff all you want, but *One Second after You Die,* you'll discover it's all true, but by then it will be too late. Therefore, to lovingly warn those who may indeed be headed in the wrong direction we're going take a look at the four classic objections that the skeptics seem to have when it comes to eternal matters. There's literally no time to waste, so let's get started.

The 1st question that skeptics seem to ask when dealing with eternal matters is the question, **"Is There Life After Death?"**

So, I ask you, *"Is There Life After Death?"*

How do we know? Well, I propose that we could start off by asking your average Joe on the street. How about the *non-Christian*? What are their beliefs on eternal matters?

- 67% of unchurched adults call themselves Christian.
- 81% believe the notion that God helps those who help themselves is taught in the Bible.
- 63% have no idea what "John 3:16" refers to, much less has the ability to quote that verse.

- 2% believe everyone is God.
- 7% believe that God is the total realization of personal, human potential.
- 2% believe that there are many gods, each with different power and authority.
- 10% believe that God is a state of higher consciousness that a person may reach.
- 2% believe that there is no such thing as God.
- 45% say that Jesus did not come back to physical life but was a great teacher.
- 51% believe that while Jesus Christ lived on earth He committed sins.
- 22% believe that Jesus Christ never got married because he was a priest and priests do not marry.
- 37% noted that there are some crimes that are unforgivable, even by God.
- 19% believe that "the whole idea of sin is outdated."
- 68% stated that Satan is merely a symbol of evil.
- 81% believe that angels exist and influence people's lives.
- 64% believe that if a person is generally good or does enough good things for others during their life, they will earn a place in Heaven.
- Only four out of ten Americans (39%) believe that "people who do not consciously accept Jesus Christ as their savior will be condemned to hell."
- There is a growing tendency to believe that all good people, whether or not they consider Jesus Christ to be their savior, will live in heaven after they die on earth.
- And recently, Pope Francis reassured atheists that, "You don't have to believe in God to go to heaven."

Well, as you can tell, the average Joe seems to be quite confused on this issue, not to mention Pope Francis. So, maybe we should ask *God's children.*

Surely, they could tell us if there is life after death! Let's now take a look at your average Christian on the street and their beliefs on eternal matters.

- 80% of Christians believe "the Bible teaches that God helps those who help themselves."
- 53% says the Holy Spirit does not exist.
- 30% says that Jesus Christ died but never had a physical resurrection.
- 29% contend that "when he lived on earth, Jesus Christ was human and committed sins like other people."
- 29% assert that "there are some crimes, sins, or other things which people which might do cannot be forgiven by God."
- 65% says that satan does not exist.
- 49% express agreement with the statement, "the devil, or Satan, is not a living being but is a symbol of evil."
- 25% agreed that it doesn't matter what faith you follow because all faith groups teach the same lessons.
- 22% agreed that all people will experience the same outcomes after death, regardless of their religious beliefs.
- 31% said that a good person can earn his/her way into heaven.
- 10% believe that they will go to heaven because basically they are a good person.
- 12% do not know what will happen to them after they die.
- 7% believe that they will go to Heaven because God loves all people and will not let them perish.
- 5% believe that when they die they will go to Heaven because they have tried to obey the 10 commandments.
- 2% believe that when they die they will not go to Heaven.

Well, as you can tell, shockingly enough, the Christian community seems to be just as confused on this issue. George Barna has this to say about the alarming status of the Church today.

"The Christian body in America is immersed in a crisis of biblical illiteracy. How else can you describe matters when most Church-going adults reject the accuracy of the Bible, reject the existence of Satan, claim that Jesus sinned, see

Research by
George Barna

no need to evangelize, believe that good works are one of the keys to persuading God to forgive their sins, and describe their commitment to Christianity as moderate or even less firm? In many ways, we are living in an age of theological anarchy."[1]

In light of this "theological anarchy," maybe we should ask those who have supposedly been there and came back. Surely, they could tell us. *Is There Life After Death?* Let's now look at a couple of people's testimonies that have had Near Death Experiences or NDE's.

"In December 1943, during World War II, twenty-year-old Dr. George Ritchie died of pneumonia. Nine minutes later, miraculously and unaccountably, he returned to life to tell of his amazing near-death experience in the afterlife.

I heard a click and a whirr. The whirr went on and on. It was getting louder. The whirr was inside my head and my knees were made of rubber. They were bending, and I was falling and all the time the whirr grew louder. I sat up with a start.

It was the first time in this entire experience that the word 'death' occurred to me in connection with what was happening. But I wasn't dead! How could I be dead and still be awake? I was me, wide awake, only without a physical body to function in. Frantically I clawed at the sheet, trying to draw it back, trying to uncover the figure on the bed. All my efforts did not even stir a breeze in the silent little room.

Now however, we seemed to have left the earth behind. And then I saw a city. A glowing, seemingly endless city, bright enough to be seen over all the unimaginable distance between. The brightness seemed to shine from the very walls and streets of this place, and from beings which I could now discern moving about within it. In fact, the city and everything in it seemed to be made of light.

At this time, I had not yet read the Book of Revelation. I could only gaze in awe at this faraway spectacle, wondering how bright each building, each inhabitant, must be. Could these radiant beings, I wondered, amazed, be those who had indeed kept Jesus the focus of their lives? Was I seeing at last, ones who had looked for Him in everything?

Seeing these beings and feeling the joy, peace, and happiness which swelled up from them made me feel that here was the place of all places, the top realm of all realms. The beings who inhabited it were full of love. This, I was and am convinced, is Heaven."[2]

Well, that man's near-death experience seemed pleasant enough. However, not all NDE's are quite that wonderful, as this next one reveals.

"On June 1, 1985, at the age of 38, Howard Storm had a near-death experience due to a perforation of the stomach and his life was forever changed.

I felt really strange, and I opened my eyes. To my surprise I was standing up next to the bed, and I was looking at my body laying in the bed. My first reaction was: 'This is crazy! I can't be standing here looking down at myself. That's not possible. Why was I still alive?' Then I heard my name. I heard: 'Howard, Howard – come here.'

Wondering, at first, where it was coming from, I discovered that it was originating in the doorway. There were different voices calling me. I asked who they were, and they said: 'We are here to take care of you. We will fix you up. Come with us.' Asking, again, who they were, I asked them if they were doctors and nurses. They responded: 'Quick, come see. You'll find out.'

With some reluctance I stepped into the hallway, and in the hallway, I was in a fog, or a haze. But the people who were calling me were 15 or 20 feet ahead, and I couldn't see them clearly. They were more like silhouettes, or shapes, and as I moved toward them they backed off into the haze. My perspective at these times was as if I were floating above the room looking down.

As we traveled, the fog got thicker and darker, and the people began to change. At first, they seemed rather playful and happy, but when we had covered some distance, a few of them began to get aggressive. The more questioning and suspicious I was, the more antagonistic and rude and authoritarian they became.

Now things got worse as I was forced by a mob of unfriendly and cruel people

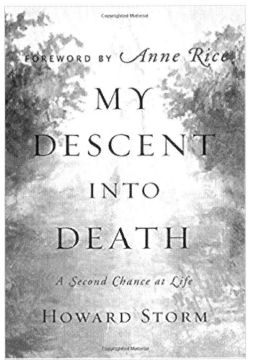

toward some unknown destination in the darkness. They began shouting and hurling insults at me, demanding that I hurry along. And they refused to answer any questions.

Finally, I told them that I wouldn't go any farther. At that time, they changed completely. They became much more aggressive and insisted that I was going with them. A number of them began to push and shove me. A wild orgy of frenzied taunting, screaming and hitting ensued. All the while it was obvious that they were having great fun.

It seemed to be almost, a game for them, with me as the center-piece of their amusement. My pain became their pleasure. They seemed to want to make me hurt –

by clawing at me and biting me. Whenever I would get one off me, there were five more to replace the one. By this time there were an innumerable host of them. Each one seemed set on coming in for the sport they got from hurting me. My attempts to fight back only provoked greater merriment."[3]

Well, even though near death experiences are fascinating, I don't think that even they can give us a definitive answer about life after death, for some of them not only contradict each other, but the Bible as well. Therefore, if we really want to know for sure, then I propose that we ask the Author of all life, God. I think He'd know, *Is There Life After Death?*

Daniel 12:1-3 "Now at that time Michael, the great prince who stands guard over the sons of your people, will arise. And there will be a time of distress such as never occurred since there was a nation until that time; and at that time your people, everyone who is found written in the book, will be rescued. Many of those who sleep in the dust of the ground will awake, these to everlasting life, but the others to disgrace and everlasting contempt. Those who have insight will shine brightly like the brightness of the expanse of heaven, and those who lead the many to righteousness, like the stars forever and ever."

This is just one of many passages in the Bible that clearly reveal the fact that when we die, we will not cease to exist. Rather, we will experience life after death in one of two places; everlasting life or everlasting contempt. In fact, the Bible teaches that when someone is buried in their grave that their souls do not stay in the ground. Rather, they go immediately upon death to the grave or the place of the departed dead also called *Sheol*. The Bible reveals that Sheol was originally the dwelling place for *both* the righteous and the unrighteous.

Psalm 9:17 "The wicked will return to Sheol, even all the nations who forget God."

So, as we can see, the wicked go to Sheol.

Psalm 30:3 "O LORD, You have brought up my soul from Sheol; You have kept me alive, that I would not go down to the pit."

However, here is a righteous person who was not going to "the pit" yet was in Sheol. So how then could the righteous and unrighteous coexist in the same place? Well, Jesus sheds light on this truth.

Luke 16:22-26 "Now the poor man died and was carried away by the angels to Abraham's bosom; and the rich man also died and was buried. In Hades he lifted up his eyes, being in torment, and saw Abraham far away and Lazarus in his bosom. And he cried out and said, 'Father Abraham, have mercy on me, and send Lazarus so that he may dip the tip of his finger in water and cool off my tongue, for I am in agony in this flame.' But Abraham said, 'Child, remember that during your life you received your good things, and likewise Lazarus bad things; but now he is being comforted here, and you are in agony. And besides all this, between us and you there is a great chasm fixed, so that those who wish to come over from here to you will not be able, and that none may cross over from there to us.'"

So, as you can see, Jesus informed us that both the righteous and unrighteous *originally* went to Sheol upon death, yet they were separated by a great chasm. Below is what *Life After Death* looked like prior to the resurrection of Jesus.

O.T. Life After Death
Sheol (Hebrew) or Hades (Greek)

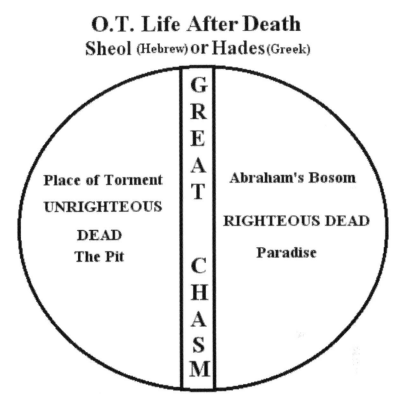

As you can see, in the Old Testament times, when people died they went to the grave or what was called Sheol. Sheol means "grave" in Hebrew. When the word grave is used in the New Testament it is called Hades. Both words are synonymous and refer to the place of the departed dead. As you can see, just as Jesus said, there exists a great chasm fixed between the two eternal destinies and neither could pass over to the other. This is how the righteous and unrighteous formally coexisted. However, after Jesus was raised from the dead, He took with Him to heaven the Old Testament righteous saints, and today, for those who give their lives to Jesus, we no longer go to a "two-sided" Sheol but go immediately to heaven.

Ephesians 4:8-10 "Therefore it says, when He ascended on high, He led captive a host of captives, and He gave gifts to men. Now this expression, He ascended, what does it mean except that He also had descended into the lower parts of the earth? He who descended is Himself also He who ascended far above all the heavens, so that He might fill all things."

2 Corinthians 12:3-4 "And I know how such a man--whether in the body or apart from the body I do not know, God knows--was caught up into Paradise and heard inexpressible words, which a man is not permitted to speak."

2 Corinthians 5:8 "We are of good courage, I say, and prefer rather to be absent from the body and to be at home with the Lord."

On the following chart is a depiction of what *Life After Death* looked like *after Jesus was raised from the dead*. This is what will happen when a person dies today.

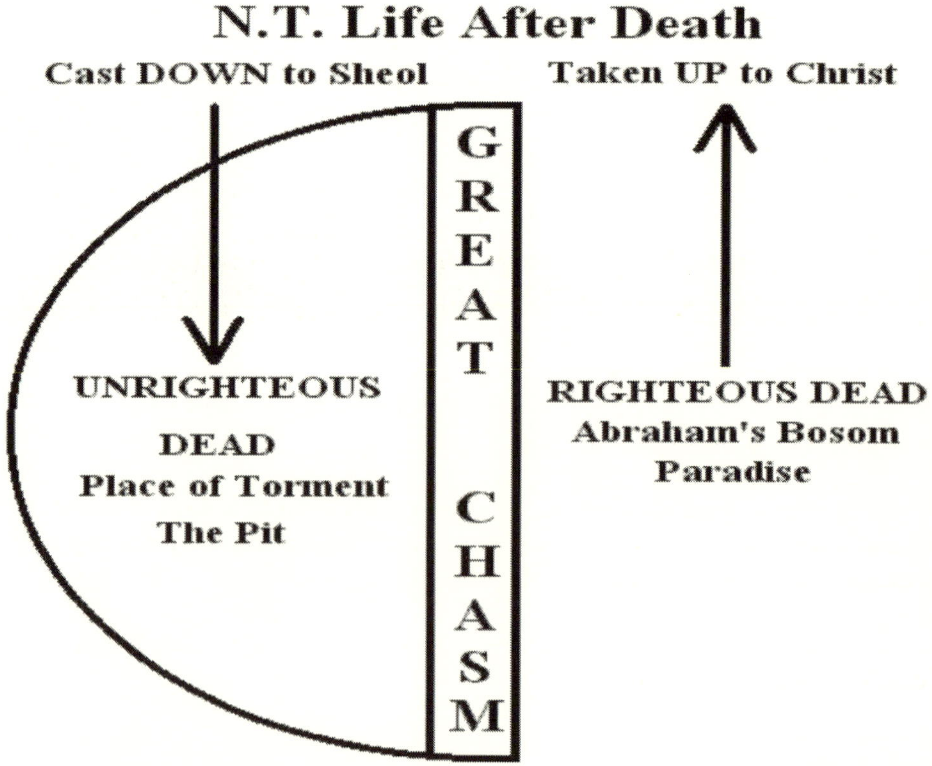

N.T. Life After Death

Cast DOWN to Sheol   **Taken UP to Christ**

G
R
E
A
T

C
H
A
S
M

UNRIGHTEOUS   **RIGHTEOUS DEAD**

DEAD   **Abraham's Bosom**
Place of Torment   **Paradise**
The Pit

Here we see that the unrighteous are still cast down to Sheol or Hades which is still a place of torment. However, after the resurrection of Jesus from the grave, the other portion of Sheol or Hades, the righteous saints, were taken up with Jesus when He ascended unto heaven. Therefore, know that Jesus is *right now* at the right hand of the Father and that as we have just read, that when the Christian leaves their body they go to be with Jesus who is with the Father in heaven, not in Sheol or Hades. Simply put, because of Jesus' sacrifice on the cross, upon death, believers now go straight to heaven while unbelievers go straight to a "one-sided" Sheol awaiting the final judgment before being cast into the Lake of Fire.

Art by Carlos S americaslastdays.blogspot.com

In fact, this issue of there really being life after death is so important in the Bible that the *whole integrity of the Gospel and Christianity* hinges on it.

1 Corinthians 15:13-14 "But if there is no resurrection of the dead, not even Christ has been raised; and if Christ has not been raised, then our preaching is vain, your faith also is vain."

Simply put, if Jesus wasn't resurrected or didn't experience life after death, then neither will we.

The **2nd thing** we need to learn about Sheol is that it **Prevents Contact with the Dead**.

And man is that a big truth needed for people to hear today! Let's clarify why you can't speak with the dead by going back to what Jesus said in Luke 16. It's so clear in there, it's not even funny.

Luke 16:24-26 "And he cried out and said, Father Abraham have mercy on me, and send Lazarus so that he may dip the tip of his finger in water and cool off my tongue for I am in agony in this flame.' But Abraham said, 'Child, remember that during your life you received your good things, and likewise Lazarus bad things; but now he is being comforted here, and you are in agony. And besides all this, between us and you there is a great chasm fixed, so that those who wish to come over from here to you will not be able, and that none may cross over from there to us.'"

So here we clearly see that once a person dies, they aren't coming back from the grave, are they? No! God has fixed a chasm so there is no crossing over back and forth, or in other words, there is no coming back! Once you're with God, you're with God. Once you're in hell. You're in hell, right? Eternal life or eternal punishment are the only options. The Bible is clear about that! And again, is this truth ever needed today or what? I mean, how many people today are getting duped by all these ghost shows or medium shows where people are supposed to be speaking with the dead?

Shows like "Ghost Hunters" or "The Long Island Medium" who are duping people into thinking that they can communicate with their dead loved one, Aunt Vera, or whoever, or some historical figure. Excuse me? That's not what the Bible says! According to the Bible, Aunt Vera or whoever died either went straight into heaven or she went straight into hell for rejecting Jesus Christ! And they've been there ever since! Why? Because there's a chasm fixed! You aren't crossing over! You aren't coming back! That's what the Bible says! If the person *did* hear a voice or saw an apparition, because I'm not saying they didn't, I'm not denying that possibility, but the Bible says it wasn't them! It's what's called a *demon* or *familiar spirit* that is deceiving you on life after death issues and leading you into occult practices. And this is precisely why God says **NOT TO DO THIS**!

Deuteronomy 18:9-14 "When you enter the land the LORD your God is giving you, do not learn to imitate the detestable ways of the nations there. Let no one be found among you who sacrifices his son or daughter in the fire, who practices divination or sorcery, interprets omens, engages in witchcraft, or casts spells, or who is a medium or spiritus, or who consults the dead. Anyone

who does these things is detestable to the LORD and because of these detestable practices the LORD your God will drive out those nations before you. You must be blameless before the LORD your God. The nations you will dispossess listen to those who practice sorcery or divination. But as for you, the LORD your God has not permitted you to do so."

Now I don't know how much clearer you can get than that, God clearly says His people are *not permitted* to speak with the dead, right? Don't even try it!

Why? Because you can't anyway, number one and two, He doesn't want you duped! He knows it opens the door to demonic deception! In fact, if you don't want to listen to God, which I don't recommend, let me give you two actual testimonies of people I know personally who violated this command from God. And when they did, things got really dark! One is a lady named Kristine from Oregon who I talked with many times and personally interviewed on this issue. The other is another good friend named Bud in Arizona and I asked both of them to write down their background and here's what they shared. Lesson learned? Don't violate the Scripture!

Kristine's Involvement in the Occult

"My father, when he was in the military got heavily involved with the occult. He said he was in a seance with some of his clan and the table started levitating and he heard voices. They all ran out of the room and these phantom things followed.

He didn't say too much more about the experience. The weird thing is he says, that a bald man sits by him at night and tells him what the kids are doing. Then there was a Ouija board at our house from my father.

Somehow, we got a hold of it and started playing with it. We would hear scratching inside the walls of the house after that and to this day that house scares the heck out of me. There is something there that is not godly."[4]

Bud's Involvement in the Occult

"Growing up I was always fascinated about the possibility of other life out there. I could not get enough about them. So, while surfing the net about them and ghost hunting, etc., I ran across a video that showed you how to make them show up on demand. It worked so well, I would invite family and friends over on weekends to witness it and we would have BBQ's and play with this.

However, it wasn't long before I started seeing dark shadows pass over me and around the yard. They were darker than the night, so dark you could see them. Hard to explain, but true. I never said anything to anyone, so they would not get scared plus I really didn't know what I was seeing.

It wasn't until a few weeks later that my second oldest daughter asked me, "Dad, what are those dark things that fly over us?" When I heard that, I just got the chills and my eyes even started to water. It was such a strange feeling because I guess I was hoping that maybe it was just me. So, I caught my breath and said, "So you see them also, huh?"

Then my youngest daughter said, "Dad I see them all over the yard and in my room." And it hit me hard because she had been telling me something would bother her at night and threw her stuffed animals at her when she was sleeping and then would hold her down.

I even slept on her floor one night to show her that there was nothing to be scared of. In fact, I set up a video camera to prove to her that nothing happens while we're sleeping. Well, I couldn't show her that video because she was right, and I was wrong.

Then one night my wife and kids took the puppies outside to let them run before bed, and my daughter ran back in telling me mom said to come and look at this. When I got outside I looked up and this huge reaper shaped thing was gliding in the air going around our house.

It looked like silk flying in the wind, but it kept circling our house. So, I walked up to about 10 feet from it and it just stared back at me. I could not see a face, but the hood was facing right at me. It was a windy full moon night and when I saw it fly in front of me I said, "God, what is that?"

We didn't talk much about it after that and still don't today. We no longer watch videos on ghost hunting, UFO's, or even scary movies, etc. We know who they are and what they want."[5]

Or in other words, we learned our lesson the hard way, don't violate the Scripture! God has fixed a chasm at the grave so there is no crossing over back and forth, and no person is coming back! Anything beyond this is a demonic apparition who is trying to dupe you into hell, the only compartment that's currently left in Sheol. They're either in heaven with God or they're in hell…period.

The **3rd thing** we need to learn about Sheol is that it's **Not the Final Destination for the Unrighteous Dead**.

Revelation 20:11-15 "Then I saw a great white throne and Him who was seated on it. Earth and sky fled from His presence, and there was no place for them. And I saw the dead, great and small, standing before the throne, and books were opened. Another book was opened, which is the book of life. The dead were judged according to what they had done as recorded in the books. The sea gave up the dead that were in it, and death and Hades gave up the dead that were in them, and each person was judged according to what he had done. Then death and Hades were thrown into the lake of fire. The lake of fire is the second death. If anyone's name was not found written in the book of life, he was thrown into the lake of fire."

　　　Now I truly believe we don't get the full impact of what's going on here in this verse until you put it all together with the timing of Sheol. Now let me see if I can picture this for you. These people did not want to trust in the work of Jesus Christ to get them to heaven and so be placed in the Book of Life. They instead trusted in their own works that were being recorded in the books, plural of works, that are recording all our deeds. And so obviously, as a result, they continued to fall short of the glory of God and were judged accordingly! Can you imagine how horrible this must be? Can you imagine how horrible a reality it must be for these people? I mean, here you are in hell and the seemingly impossible has just happened. BOOM! You're out of there! You've been tormented day after day, year after year, in total agony in flames of torment, you're weeping and gnashing your teeth, when all of a sudden POOF! You're out of that intense horrible never-ending agony standing before God in a pain free, blessed environment. Think of the emotion! You actually get a reprieve thinking, "Praise God I made it out!" And there you are starting to fill up with joy and relief when the words ring out, "Since you did not want to trust in the work of my Son Jesus Christ on the cross, and instead trusted in your own works, you will now be cast into the Lake of Fire forever and ever and ever!" They went from the frying pan, into the fire! Can you imagine that?

Now here's my point. I don't know about you, but it sure appears to me that the Bible is absolutely emphatic that there really is Life After Death, even down to the nitty gritty, you know what I'm saying? In fact, let me clue you in on something. It's all over the place. From cover to cover! Why? Because God loves us and He's trying to get us prepared for that which lasts forever! It's called eternity! And that's why the Scriptures exist, not so we can get the right answer on Jeopardy, but so we can be adequately prepared for eternity! There really is life after death! You can count on it! So, the question you must ask yourself as you're reading this is, are you ready for the journey? Have you made adequate preparations? The sad thing is that most people are just plain too busy making other plans. Erwin Lutzer reveals this sad truth.

"Recently, I read a tragic story about people enjoying themselves on the top stories of a tall apartment building not knowing that there was a fire burning on

the lower floors. Just so, many are enjoying life, comfortably ignoring the fact that their death is not only inevitable, but much nearer then they think.

Though there are many uncertainties in our lives, we can count on this: Whatever we strive for in this world must, of necessity, be temporary. Indeed, this world and all we have accumulated will eventually be burned up.

The other day I was browsing in a travel section of a bookstore. Potential travelers were buying maps and guidebooks on Hawaii and Europe. Some were purchasing booklets to help them learn some phrases of a foreign language. No doubt they had saved their money, blocked out their vacation schedules, and purchased airline tickets.

All that just for a two-week journey. I wondered how many of them were giving at least that much attention to their final destination. I wondered how many were reading the guidebook, studying the map, and trying to learn the language of heaven. Europe and Hawaii seemed so much more real than the unseen realm of the dead. And yet, even as they planned their vacations, they were en route to a more distant destination.

If we are wise, we will spend our time preparing for that which lasts forever. What is life but preparation for eternity."[6]

Did you know that you are going to be dead a lot longer then you are alive? You are you know. Each one of us is going to make that journey, some sooner than others. Are you sure that if you were to die today, that you'd go to heaven and not hell? Well, if you're reading this and you're not sure, then don't delay. Once you're gone, you're not coming back and there is no second chance. Please, I encourage you today, give your life to Jesus *now*, while He may still be found. God loves you and has made provision for you to spend eternal bliss with Him. But you must make that eternal decision that _will_ decide your ultimate destiny.

Is There Life After Death? Yes, there is. So please, give your heart to Jesus *now*. Don't leave this earth without Him. Reach out and accept His forgiveness of your sins. Why? Because *One Second After You Die*, it's going to be too late!

Chapter Two

What Happens When You Die?

"One day there was this minister that died, and he was waiting in line at the Pearly Gates. And ahead of him he saw this guy who was dressed in sunglasses, a loud shirt, leather jacket, and jeans.

So, Saint Peter addresses this guy with the loud shirt and jeans and says, 'Who are you, so that I may know whether or not to admit you into the Kingdom of Heaven?'

And the guy replies, 'I'm Joe Cohen, taxi-driver, of New Yawk City.'

So, Saint Peter consults his list and he smiles and joyfully says to the taxi- driver, 'Take this silken robe and golden staff and enter the Kingdom of Heaven.'

The taxi-driver goes into Heaven with his robe and staff.

Well now it's the minister's turn. So, he stands tall and booms out, 'I am Peter Finnster, Pastor of Saint Michael's for the last forty-three years.'

Saint Peter consults his list and casually says to the minister, 'Oh, alright, take this cotton robe and wooden staff and enter the Kingdom of Heaven.'

But the minister objects and says, 'Now, just wait a minute here. That man was a taxi-driver and he gets a silken robe and golden staff. I'm a preacher but I get a cotton robe and a wooden one? How can this be?'

And Saint Peter replied, 'Well you see Pastor, up here we work by results. While you preached, people slept; while he drove, people prayed.'"

Now how many of you can identify with that sleeping part, you know what I'm saying? Sleeping while the preacher preached. Here's my point. What's really not funny about that joke is this. It reminds me how people today actually think we can somehow earn our way to heaven, when the Bible clearly teaches that Jesus Christ is the *only* way to heaven! And here's the point. You can scoff all you want, but *One Second After You Die*, you'll discover, just like that, it was all true, every last bit of it, but now it's too late.

The **2nd objection** that skeptics come up with is this: If there really is life after death, **"What Happens When You Die?"**

Once again, this is a logical, great straightforward question. I mean, stop think about it. If all this Jesus stuff is true, and there really is a heaven and there really is a hell, and there really is life after death, then can we know for sure exactly what happens at the moment of death? I mean, can we really know for sure what happens not if, but when we die? Of course! God doesn't leave us hanging high and dry! The Bible's not just specific about there being life after death. It's extremely specific about what life's going to be like for us after death. But that's right, before we do that, we need to first dispel some of the false teachings out there concerning the afterlife.

The **1ˢᵗ false teaching** concerning the afterlife is **The Theory of Evolution**.

But don't take my word for it. Let's listen to God's.

Romans 1:18-22 "The wrath of God is being revealed from heaven against all the godlessness and wickedness of men who suppress the truth by their wickedness, since what may be known about God is plain to them, because God has made it plain to them. For since the creation of the world God's invisible qualities – His eternal power and divine nature – have been clearly seen, being understood from what has been made, so that men are without excuse. For although they knew God, they neither glorified Him as God nor gave thanks to Him, but their thinking became futile and their foolish hearts were darkened. Although they claimed to be wise, they became fools."

Now according to our text, the Bible is clear. Nobody, and I mean nobody, is going to die and stand before God and say, "Hey God, you can't send me to hell. I mean, come on man, that's not fair! I just didn't have enough proof that you existed." Are you kidding me? What did it say there? No one, that's right, no one, is without excuse before God because God made His existence known through the complexity or design of His creation, right? In other words, you and I should be able to look at a flea, a tree, a bee or you and me and say, "Wow! Look at all that design. That couldn't happen by chance. Why, there must be a God and I better get right with Him before it's too late," right? Of course! That's the wise conclusion. In fact, if you don't want to listen to God, which I don't recommend,

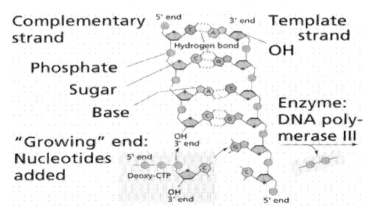

then maybe you should listen to modern day scientists. Even they are admitting that there's no such thing as a "simple cell" as evolution would say. Rather it's a complex well-designed machine factory. It is absolutely mind boggling to say that the so-called "simple cell" evolved by chance! There is no simple cell! That's ludicrous! The supposed simplest cell of all, the paramecium, is more complex than the space shuttle!

And our DNA molecule is the most complex molecule in the universe. Its code is so unbelievably complex that if you typed it all out it would create enough books to fill the Grand Canyon 40 times. In fact, our bodies have 50 trillion cells, with each cell having 46 chromosomes, but if you took all of the chromosomes out of your body, they'd only fill up 2 tablespoons! And if you stretched them out and tied them all together, one person's chromosomes would reach from the earth to the moon and back, FIVE MILLION times! Yet evolution comes along and says there is no God and there is no afterlife. I'm sorry, you have to have more faith to believe in THAT than the Biblical account! That's what the facts say! The SCIENTIFIC facts! And then on top of that, evolution not only gets it wrong on the existence of God, but then they say that when we die we just go back to the ground to become worm bait, right? That's what's being taught in school! But that's not what the Bible says. It says we were created in the image of God and therefore just like God we are going to continue to exist forever!

1 Corinthians 15:51-53 "Listen, I tell you a mystery: We will not all sleep,

but we will all be changed— in a flash, in the twinkling of an eye, at the last trumpet. For the trumpet will sound, the dead will be raised imperishable, and we will be changed. For the perishable must clothe itself with the imperishable, and the mortal with immortality."

According to our text, the Bible is clear. When we die, we are not going to go back to the ground to become worm bait. Are you kidding me? In the twinkling of an eye, we're going to put on immortality and continue to exist in one of two places. And people, you can scoff all you want, but just like that, at the moment you die, you'll discover just how foolish evolution really was. You were lied to! But by then, it will be too late.

The **2nd false teaching** concerning the afterlife is **The Theory of Little gods**.

That's right, believe it or not, there are actually people out there who really believe that at the moment we die, we get to become little gods and our wives become little goddesses who then forever get to be pregnant and populate planets throughout the universe! And that's right, for some reason, my wife doesn't want to do that. But seriously, anyone using their brain can see that this is a *logical absurdity*. How can a being that had a beginning (i.e you and I) become God who by definition *never* had a beginning? How can a being that was created ever become a being Who by definition was never created? That's not just illogical. It's unbiblical.

Isaiah 43:10 "You are my witnesses, declares the LORD, before me no god was formed, nor will there be one after me."

Isaiah 44:6,8 "This is what the LORD says – I am the first and I am the last; apart from me there is no God. Is there any God besides me? No, there is no other Rock; I know not one."

Isaiah 45:5 "I am the LORD, and there is no other; apart from me there is no God."

The Bible is clear. When you die, you will not become a god, let alone realize all of a sudden you were one. You'll have a realization alright. You'll realize there is only One God, just like the Bible says, to Whom you're going to have to give an account. But by then it will be too late.

The **3rd false teaching** concerning the afterlife is **The Theory of Reincarnation**.

Now this is one of the most popular false teachings out there concerning the afterlife. And what reincarnation would have you and I believe, is that when we die, we just get recycled into many different beings throughout many different lifetimes. And then supposedly based upon what we did in one life will reflect in our existence in another life. For instance, they say if I was mean and rotten to other people in one life then I'll come back in the next one as a person who is treated mean and rotten by other people. And they call this the "law of karma." And then to make matters worse, they even go so far as to say that the Bible teaches reincarnation based on a misunderstanding of this verse.

John 3:3 "In reply Jesus declared, I tell you the truth, no one can see the kingdom of God unless he is born again."

Uh oh, well folks there you have it. You must be born again. Reincarnation is true. Wrong answer! First of all, notice it did not say, born again and again and again, as reincarnation would imply. And second, the context clearly reveals that it's talking about "spiritual" birth not "physical"! Which is exactly why Nicodemus said, "Hey wait a minute Jesus, I can't go back into my mother's womb? I can't have a second physical birth." And that's exactly why Jesus says, "You're right. You have to be born of the Spirit. I'm talking about a 'spiritual birth' not a physical one!" And that's exactly why the Bible *does not* teach the "law of karma" but rather the "Law of Jehovah" which says we live only once and after that, we are going to face judgment.

Hebrews 9:27 "And inasmuch as it is appointed for men to die once and after this comes judgment."

You can scoff all you want, but when you die, you're not coming back as a worm, a flea, a tree, or another you and me. Rather, you're going to stand before Almighty God in His Presence in eternity! And you'll be judged for every single thing you did on this earth. Therefore, the point is this. You better get it right with Him *the first and the only time*.

The **4th false teaching** concerning the afterlife is **The Theory of Soul Sleep**.

What people here would have you and I believe is that when we die, we just take a "big cosmic nap" in the sky. We just go into some sort of soul sleep where we await the day that we're resurrected. And again, just like reincarnation, it's based on yet another misunderstanding of Scripture that talks about those who have "fallen asleep."

Thessalonians 4:15 "According to the Lord's own word, we tell you that we who are still alive, who are left till the coming of the Lord, will certainly not precede those who have fallen asleep."

Oh no, there you have it! When we die we turn into the ultimate couch potato and we just fall asleep. Wrong answer! The term "fallen asleep" here is not a literal sleep. You don't turn into a cosmic couch potato when you die. Falling asleep is a common phrase the Bible uses to describe death, because a dead body appears to be asleep. And we'll get to those other common phrases the Bible uses in a minute. But even so, the Bible is clear.

When we die as a Christian, we will not go to sleep. But rather we will go straight to be with Jesus Who's *also* not asleep!

2 Corinthians 5:8 "We are of good courage, I say, and prefer rather to be absent from the body and to be at home with the Lord."

Philippians 1:23 "I am torn between the two: I desire to depart and be with Christ, which is better by far."

Jesus isn't sleeping, and neither will we! And if you want further proof, then look no further than Matthew 17 at the transfiguration of Jesus where Moses and Elijah were alive, speaking with Jesus, not taking a nap. And previously we saw in Luke 16 with the parable of the rich man and Lazarus, who were not only alive, but clearly speaking, remembering, and were either in agony or comfort, depending on their location. No sleeping! The Bible is clear. You can scoff all you want, but Jesus isn't taking a "cosmic nap" and neither will we. Absent from the body is to be present with the Lord, *if you're a Christian*. But the point is this. If you're not, you'll be present alright. You'll be present in a place called hell.

The **5th and final false teaching** concerning the afterlife is **The Theory of Purgatory**.

Now what this false teaching would have you and I believe is that when we die, we don't go to be with Jesus. No! They say we go to some sort of "holding pen" where we purge our sins through fire and suffering so we can hopefully make it to heaven someday. And you might be thinking, "Well come on, people don't really believe that today, do they? I mean, that's an old Catholic teaching, they don't believe in that anymore, do they?" Well, you might want to ask Pope Francis. He not only still believes in it apparently, but he even stated that for those who listened to his latest live broadcast on Twitter, they could shave off some time in purgatory. Can you believe that? And again, what makes this one even worse is that people *assume* purgatory is taught in the Bible, yet there's *not one single passage* in the Bible that supports it! And second, this is a slap in the face to the atonement of Christ, which says that Jesus' sacrifice on the cross is sufficient payment for *all* our sins. But apparently, according to purgatory, when Jesus said it was finished on the cross, it wasn't really finished! Apparently, we have to now finish the job for Him by our own suffering, even suffering through a lecture by the Pope on Twitter! Excuse me? People, that's not just ludicrous, it's blasphemous! The Bible clearly says that when Jesus Christ died on the cross, He died for *all* our sins, for *all* time, every last one of them! I didn't say that. God did!

Hebrews 10:14 "For by one offering He has perfected for all time those who are sanctified."

The Bible is clear. There are no sins we can ever "purge" in order to get to heaven. Jesus Christ bore them on the cross and it's the acceptance of *His work*, is how we get into heaven. And you can scoff all you want, but if you really think you've got to do something to add to what Jesus did, *you've got a false salvation.* You're not going to heaven. You're going straight to hell. I didn't say that. Jesus did! But that's right, that's the bad false teachings concerning the afterlife. Now let's turn to the good, true teachings of the afterlife, that is, for *the Christian*. Here's what the Christian can expect when they die.

The **1st way** the Bible likens death for a Christian is a **Pleasant Transition**.

Luke 9:28-31 "About eight days after Jesus said this, He took Peter, John and James with Him and went up onto a mountain to pray. As He was praying, the appearance of His face changed, and His clothes became as bright as a flash of lightning. Two men, Moses and Elijah, appeared in glorious splendor, talking with Jesus. They spoke about His departure, which He was about to bring to fulfillment at Jerusalem."

Now according to our text, the Greek word for "departure" here is where we get the word "exodus" from. So, the picture that's painted here for us, is that just as Moses led the Israelites out of bondage from Egypt, so our Lord Jesus Christ has departed *first* through death's door, and He will now lead us out into the eternal promised land called heaven. Therefore, the Christian does not need to be anxious or distraught about our departure because Jesus will Personally take us there to a place called heaven. The eternal promised land.

The **2ⁿᵈ way** the Bible likens death for a Christian is as a **Sailing** Ship.

Philippians 1:23 "But I am hard-pressed from both directions, having the desire to depart and be with Christ, for that is very much better."

Now again, the Greek word here Paul uses for "depart" is different than the one we just saw. This one literally means "the loosing of an anchor." It's actually a shipping term. Therefore, the picture that is painted for us here is that upon death, when our loved ones are still saying their goodbyes, and we've loosed our anchors to this earth, and we've sailed away to the other horizon, that there will be a host of other heavenly beings on the other horizon, welcoming us to our new eternal home. And that's why death for the Christian is not so much the final voyage, as it is the final Welcome Home.

The **3ʳᵈ way** the Bible likens death for the Christian is as a **Restful** Sleep.

Luke 8:52 "Now they were all weeping and lamenting for her; but He said, "Stop weeping, for she has not died, but is asleep."

Now as we saw before, this is not speaking of a "soul sleep." Again, it's just a way the Bible likens death for the Christian. It's as if "we did go to sleep" but we instantly wake up and go to be with Jesus as we saw. And when you understand this, it really brings this amazing truth home. For instance, how many of you have been really, really tired? Or maybe had a rotten night's sleep followed by a long and extremely exhausting day and you just couldn't wait to get home and go to bed? Well, this is the picture that's painted for us here, that when a person who has made Jesus their Shepherd dies, we leave this tired ol' body and the earth behind as if we went to sleep, only to discover that we have awakened in the restful arms of our wonderful Lord Jesus. In fact, it's almost as if you've stepped from one room into the next like it was with this boy.

From the Movie "A Man Called Peter":

"In a home of which I know, a little boy, the only son, was ill with an incurable disease. Month after month the mother had tenderly nursed him, read to him, and

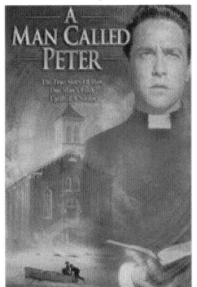

played with him, hoping to keep him from the dreadful finality of the doctor's diagnosis – the little boy was sure to die.

One day his mother was reading him a story and after she closed the book her little son sat silent for an instant, deeply stirred. Then he asked the question weighing on his childish heart, 'Mama, what is it like to die? Mama, does it hurt?'

Quick tears sprang to her eyes and she fled to the kitchen, supposedly to tend to something on the stove. She knew it was a question with deep significance. She knew it must be answered satisfactorily.

So, she breathed a hurried prayer that the Lord would keep her from breaking down before the boy, and that she would be able to tell him the answer the Lord did tell her. Immediately she knew how to explain it to him.

'Kenneth,' she said to her son, 'do you remember when you were a tiny boy, how you used to play so hard all day, that when night came you were too tired to even undress and you'd tumble into your mother's bed and fall asleep? That was not your bed, it was not where you belonged.

You would only stay there a little while. Much to your surprise you would wake up and find yourself in your own bed in your own room. You were there because someone had loved you and taken care of you. Your father had come with big strong arms and carried you away.'

'Kenneth darling, death is just like that. We just wake up some morning to find ourselves in the other room. Our room where we belong, because the Lord Jesus loved us and died for us.'

The lad's shining face looking up into hers told her that the point had gone home and there would be no more fear and he never questioned again. And several weeks later he fell asleep just as she said, and he was carried into his own room by his Heavenly Father."[1]

Just like that story reveals, the Bible declares that at the transition from this world into the next, we shall be changed, in the twinkling of an eye. And through Jesus, God will not only take us to heaven, but in our final hour, oftentimes, He'll even take us there Personally. It's a wonderful transition, if Jesus is your Personal Shepherd.

The **4th way** the Bible likens death for a Christian is as a **Collapsing Tent.**

2 Corinthians 5:1 "For we know that if the earthly tent which is our house is torn down, we have a building from God, a house not made with hands, eternal in the heavens."

Now if you look around, you'll notice that some of our tents here today are pretty torn and tattered, some worse than others but we won't go there. And what's going on here is the text is talking about our earthly tents, i.e. our bodies. So, the picture that's painted for us here is that there will come a day when the Christian's body, i.e. our tents are just simply going to pull up stakes. And then we're going to head off not to another dusty ol' campground here on earth. We're going to a mansion that awaits us in heaven prepared by God Himself. I don't know about you, but granted, camping is cool, but man, there's nothing like being home with all the amenities, you know what I'm saying? Now here's the point. Can you imagine all the amenities that await us in our heavenly home? It's going to be awesome!

The **5th and final way** the Bible likens death for a Christian is just that, a **Permanent Home**.

John 14:2-3 "In My Father's house are many dwelling places; if it were not so, I would have told you; for I go to prepare a place for you. If I go and prepare a place for you, I will come again and receive you to Myself, that where I am, there you may be also."

Now according to our text, this is amazing. How many of you have ever worried about your home where you live, you know what I'm saying? I mean, there always seems to be something concerning us about our homes, right? Whether it's bugs to kill, bills to pay, or the thing burning down. It's always something, right? Oh, but according to our text, *not so for the Christian.* The picture that is painted for us here is that there will come a day when we'll never have to worry about our home ever again. Why? Because our heavenly home will not only be totally decked out, it's going to be totally permanent. And that's why, contrary to what society says, heaven is a real place and you really don't want to miss it, like this man shares.

The following is an actual testimony of a Christian Pastor who died in a car accident, and he tells us what he saw, before he was miraculously revived. Take it for what it is, here's what he said he experienced.

"When I died, I didn't flow through a long, dark tunnel, I had no sense of fading away or of coming back. I never felt my body being transported into the light. I heard no voices calling to me or anything else.

In my next moment of awareness, I was standing I heaven.

Joy pulsated through me as I looked around, and at that moment I became aware of a large crowd of people. They stood in front of a brilliant, ornate gate. As they surged toward me, I knew instantly that all of them had died during my lifetime.

They rushed toward me, and every person was smiling, shouting, and praising God. Although no one said so, intuitively I knew they were my celestial welcoming committee. It was as if they had all gathered just outside heaven's gate, waiting for me.

I still didn't know why, but the joyousness of the place wiped away any questions. Everything felt blissful. Perfect. Everything I experienced was like a first-class buffet for the senses. I had never felt such powerful embraces or feasted my eyes on such beauty.

Never, even in my happiest moments, had I ever felt so fully alive. I stood speechless in front of the crowd of loved ones, still trying to take in everything. Over and over I heard how overjoyed they were to see me and how excited they were to have me among them.

I felt loved – more than ever before in my life. When they gazed at me, I knew what the Bible means by perfect love. It emanated from every person who surrounded me. All were full of life and expressed radiant joy. Heaven was many things, but without a doubt, it was the greatest family reunion of all.

I was home; I was where I belonged. I wanted to be there more than I had ever wanted to be anywhere on earth. Time had slipped away, and I was simply present in heaven. I had no needs. I felt perfect. All worries, all anxieties, and all concerns had simply vanished.[2]

Now again, I don't recommend building your theology on a Near Death Experience, even a Christian one, but it sure seems to me, there's a pattern here for the Christian. Our heavenly home is going to be pretty awesome! And here's the point. How many different ways and how many different times does God have to try to get it through our heads? Heaven is real, and you really don't want to miss it! I mean, can you imagine how awesome it's going to be? If it only took God six days to create the whole universe and all of life that we see, can you imagine what kind of place Jesus has been preparing for us for nearly 2,000 years? It's going to make this place look like a garbage can! People, I beg you, there really is a heaven and there really is a hell. And so, I ask you, "Are you ready for the journey? Are you sure if you were to die today, that you'd go to heaven and not hell? Scoff all you want, but one day you're going to die and there's nothing you can do to stop it. And so, I ask you please give your life to Jesus now because *One Second After You Die*, it's going to be too late. But don't listen to me, listen to Jesus.

John 14:6 "I am the way, and the truth, and the life. No one comes to the Father except through Me."

What Happens When We Die?

Well, it all depends on what you do with Jesus' statement here. Again, notice that Jesus didn't say that He was one of the many ways, one of the many truths, or even one of the many avenues of life. He was very clear in what He told us, that He is the *only* way, the *only* truth, and the *only* life. People, if there is one thing that you do not want to get wrong, it is where you will spend eternity. Our last breath here is our first breath in either heaven or hell. So, the question you must ask yourself is, "Are you ready for the journey? Have you made adequate preparations? Are you sure that if you were to die today, that you'd go to heaven and not hell?" Well, if you're reading this and you're not sure, then don't delay. Once you're gone, you're not coming back and there is no second chance. Please, I encourage you today, give your life to Jesus *now*, while He may still be found. God loves you and has made a wonderful provision for you to spend eternal bliss with Him in heaven. But you must make that eternal decision that *will* decide your ultimate destiny. Please, give your heart to Jesus. Reach out and accept His love and forgiveness of your sins before its too late. Don't leave this earth without Him. Why? Because *One Second After You Die*, it's going to be too late!

Chapter Three

Is There Really A Hell?

"A stingy old guy who had been diagnosed with a terminal illness was determined to prove wrong the saying, "You can't take it with you." After much thought and consideration, the old miser finally figured out how to take at least some of his money with him when he died.

He instructed his wife to go to the bank and withdraw enough money to fill two pillow cases. He then directed her to take the bags of money to the attic and leave them directly above his bed. His plan was that when he passed away, he would reach out and grab the bags on his way to heaven.

Well, several weeks after the funeral, the deceased man's wife was up in the attic cleaning when she came upon the two forgotten pillow cases stuffed with cash.

She exclaimed, "Oh, that old fool. I knew he should have had me put the money in the basement."

Now maybe it's just me, but how many of you would say that guy learned the hard way you can't take it with you when you die? In fact, it doesn't even matter where you put it, in the attic or the basement, you're still not going to take it with you because the Bible says in the Book of Job, "Naked you came into this world and naked you're going out." And here's the point. Even though the statistics on death are pretty amazing, "One out of every one people die", people today still act like its no big deal and assume there's no danger. Yet, the Bible clearly says you really are going up through the attic to heaven, or you're going down through the basement straight to hell! Scoff all you want, but *One Second After You Die*, you'll discover just like that, it was all true, every last bit of it, but now it's too late.

The **3ʳᵈ objection** that skeptics come up with is this: If there really is life after death and we really are going someplace when we die then, "**Is There Really a Hell?**"

And once again, this is a logical, great straightforward question. I mean, stop and think about it. If all this Jesus stuff is true, and there really is life after death, and when we die we really are going to one of two places, then is one of those places really a place of eternal torment? I mean, is there really a hell? Of course! But don't take my word for it. Let's listen to God's.

Luke 16:19-31 "There was a rich man who was dressed in purple and fine linen and lived in luxury every day. At his gate was laid a beggar named Lazarus, covered with sores and longing to eat what fell from the rich man's table. Even the dogs came and licked his sores. The time came when the beggar died, and the angels carried him to Abraham's side. The rich man also died and was buried. In hell, where he was in torment, he looked up and saw Abraham far away, with Lazarus by his side. So, he called to him, 'Father Abraham, have pity on me and send Lazarus to dip the tip of his finger in water and cool my tongue, because I am in agony in this fire.' But Abraham replied, 'Son, remember that in your lifetime you received your good things, while Lazarus received bad things, but now he is comforted here, and you are in agony. And besides all this, between us and you a great chasm has been fixed, so that those who want to go from here to you cannot, nor can anyone cross over from there to us.' He answered, 'Then I beg you, send Lazarus to my father's house, for I have five brothers. Let him warn them, so that they will not also come to this place of torment.' Abraham replied, 'They have Moses and the Prophets; let them listen to them.' 'No, father Abraham,' he said, 'but if someone from the dead goes to them, they will repent.' He said to him, 'If they do not listen to Moses and the Prophets, they will not be convinced even if someone rises from the dead.'"

Now as you can clearly see, it's quite obvious that a place of eternal torment really does exist. And keep in mind, we just read an account concerning the existence of hell from Who? From Jesus Himself, right? In fact, if you look at the Gospels, you will find that Jesus spoke more about eternal punishment and hell than He did about heaven. In fact, He was very graphic about it.

"The word hell translates from Gehenna, the Greek form of the Hebrew phrase that means 'the vale of Hinnom'—a valley west and south of Jerusalem. In this valley, the Canaanites worshiped Baal and the god Molech by sacrificing their children in a fire that burned continuously.

In the time of Jesus, the Valley of Hinnom was used as the garbage dump of Jerusalem. Into it were thrown all the filth and garbage of the city, including the dead bodies of animals and executed criminals.

To consume all this, fires burned constantly. Maggots worked in the filth. When the wind blew from that direction over the city, its awfulness was quite evident. At night wild dogs howled as they fought over the garbage.

Jesus used this awful scene as a symbol of hell. In effect He said, 'Do you want to know what hell is like? Look at Gehenna.'

So, hell may be described as God's 'cosmic garbage dump.' All that is unfit for heaven will be thrown into hell."[1]

Now I don't know about you, but I'd say Jesus considered hell a very important topic, and He was very graphic about it. Oh, but that's the tip of the iceberg. The Bible is emphatic about how horrible of a place this is. You definitely don't want to go there! Let's take a look.

- Place of Thirst: (Luke 16)

- Place of Worms: (Mark 9)
- Place of No Return: (Luke 16)
- Place of Remembrance: (Luke 16)
- Place of the Wicked Dead: (Luke 10)

- Place of the Wicked Demons: (2 Peter 2)
- Place of a Bottomless Pit: (Luke 8)
- Place of a Burning Waste Dump: (Matt. 23)
- Place of Outer Darkness: (Matt. 8)
- Place of Fire: (Rev. 20)
- Place of the Lake of Fire: (Rev. 20)
- Place of Eternal Fire: (Matt. 18)
- Place of Unquenchable Fire: (Mark 9)
- Place of Everlasting Punishment: (Matt. 25)
- Place of Eternal Condemnation: (Mark 3)
- Place of Eternal Judgment: (Heb. 6)
- Place of Everlasting Destruction: (2 Thess. 1)
- Place of Weeping & Gnashing of Teeth: (Matt. 13)
- Place of Torment: (Luke 16)
- Place of Eternal Torment: (Rev. 20)

Now maybe it's just me, but I'm kind of thinking hell is the last place you ever want to be, you know what I'm saying? Therefore, is it any wonder that Jesus talked about hell twice as much as He did about heaven? Of course not! Any sane person would warn others of going to a place like that, right? And herein lies the problem. Jesus and the Bible repeat many times that there really is a hell, and you really don't want to go there, people still refuse to believe and even throw up various objections at its existence.

And the **1st objection** to Hell that people come up with to hell is called **Universalism**.

And what universalism would have you and I believe is that everybody will universally get saved regardless of their actions or beliefs and thus nobody goes to hell because there's no need for one. But if this were true, then why do we need to share the gospel? I mean, if everybody's going to heaven then why evangelize? But the truth is, Jesus *did tell us to evangelize*, right? And furthermore, if universalism is true then wouldn't this mean that the devil himself will eventually go to heaven? Yet, the Bible says that Jesus came to destroy the works of the devil, not to save him. And besides, universalism denies the clear teaching we've already seen about two eternal places, heaven and hell, not just one.

The **2nd objection** people come up with to hell, is that if there is a hell, **it's only temporary.**

You see, some people think that those who end up in hell will somehow, someway, eventually, be able to get out. They say it's just too harsh to be tormented forever. But that's not what the Bible says.

Matthew 25:46 "Then they will go away to eternal punishment, but the righteous to eternal life."

Now you can't get anymore cut and dried than that. How long is eternal life? Forever, right? Therefore, in the exact same text there, "How long is eternal punishment?" Just as long isn't it? People, *hell is not temporary*. It's just as forever as heaven is forever.

The **3rd objection** to hell is called **Annihilationism**.

Since people can't deny the texts that clearly reveal that hell exists, they once again try to soften the harshness of God's retribution by saying something like this. "Well, if hell does exist, then people who go there don't suffer endlessly. No! They simply cease to be or in other words they're annihilated." But that's not what the Bible says.

Revelation 20:7,10 "When the thousand years are over, Satan will be released from his prison. And the devil, who deceived them, was thrown into the lake of burning sulfur, where the beast and the false prophet had been thrown. They will be tormented day and night for ever and ever."

Now according to our text, it's pretty obvious that the beast and the false prophet haven't been annihilated there in hell, have they? No! *They're still alive* suffering torment in hell after being there for 1,000 years! Besides, annihilation would not be a punishment, it would be a *release from punishment*. And since the Bible declares that hell is a place of punishment, annihilation can't be true.

The **4th objection** to hell is that **Hell is life on earth. Besides, if there is a hell, I'll get to party with all my buddies.**

Anybody who makes this statement has obviously never read the Bible. They've obviously never studied what hell is like. And I personally like Dr. Mal Couch's study on hell:

"Picture a time that just continues to tumble on and on forever, never ending, never slowing down, the same years and decades of torment, regret, sorrow, pain, blanketed darkness, nights never ending, constant consciousness, lostness, aloneness, loneliness, rumblings from the pit, groans, torturing fire, choking smells, unending and unending, no

letting-up, no relief, no comfort, never resting, never ceasing, never relenting, no end in sight, one hundred years rolling into another one hundred years, slowly turning over into a thousand years, painstakingly evolving into another thousand years, and finally into a million years, the same grinding pain, the continual bone- racking agony, screams upon screams, weeping upon weeping, echoing sighs upon sighs!"[2]

Now maybe it's just me, but if that's your idea of a party, I'm not going. I don't care how many times you invite me. So, the point is this. Those who end up in hell will wish it was only as bad as life on earth. And I guarantee you, there won't be any partying.

The **5th objection** to hell is that **Only "rotten" people go to hell**.

This is actually one of the biggest lies from the pit of hell! You see, the

Bible teaches that *all people* are currently headed for hell and that there is *no neutral position*.

John 8:42,44 "Jesus told them, If God were your Father, you would love me, because I have come to you from God. For you are the children of your father the devil, and you love to do the evil things he does."

The Bible is clear. We either belong to God or we belong to who? The devil, right? There is no "middle road." We are all considered rotten because of our rotten sin! And we only cease to become a child of the devil and become a child of God when we get saved. Not one second sooner, not one second later. And how ironic it is that those who think there's a "neutral" position out there, not only still belong to the devil, but they're *still on the way to hell*. And gee, I'd say that's a pretty good trick of the devil, how about you?

The **6th objection** to hell is that **Hell is unfair.** A good and loving God would never allow for such a place.

Now that sounds so wonderful but its absolutely unbiblical. You see, it's precisely *because God is good* that He *must* judge all. God must punish wickedness, otherwise He couldn't be loving or good. Would it be loving if God allowed people to get away with the murder, rape, torture, etc. that we all know never makes it to court or even gets found out? Would it be loving or good for God to allow Hitler or the 911 terrorists to enjoy eternal bliss in heaven without having to deal with their wicked deeds? How loving is that? And it's precisely because God is good and loving that He not only will judge all, but He's also provided a way of out of it. And remember, He didn't have to. Therefore, the point is this. Throw up any objection you want, but if you're going to be true to the Scripture or the Word of Jesus, you cannot deny the existence of a hell. There really is one and you really don't want to go! Oh, but it gets worse. It's one thing for the world to deny the existence of hell. I can understand that. I didn't want to believe in it either before I got saved. But now even *the Church* is denying the existence of hell! And how sick is it for people to know there is a hell, but refuse to warn other people about it? It reminds me of what an atheist said one time:

"An atheist said to a Christian, 'If I believed what you Christians say you believe about a coming judgment, and that rejecters of Christ will be lost eternally in hell, then I would crawl on my bare knees on crushed glass all over the city, warning men, night and day, to flee from the coming day of God's wrath!"

But, before you cop on those spineless churches who refuse to lovingly warn people that there really is a hell and you really don't want to go there, you need to ask yourself, are you doing the same thing by making excuses or padding the terminology of hell.

The 1st phrase people come up with to try to soften hell is, "Hey, you don't want to have a **Christless Eternity,** do you?

Excuse me? A "Christless Eternity?" What's that? What does a "Christless Eternity" mean to a person who's lost? They don't know Christ and they think they're fine. That's their problem! How does a "Christless Eternity" help them realize that unless they get right with God, through Christ, they're going straight to hell? Answer? They don't! It's hampering the Gospel, not helping it!

The 2nd phrase people come up with to try to soften hell is, "Hey man, **don't you want to go to heaven?"**

Well duh, of course people want to go to heaven! Who doesn't want to go to heaven? In fact, again, this is their problem. Most people think they're going to heaven. Yet, Jesus Christ is the only way to heaven and if they don't have Him, they're going where? They're going to hell! I didn't say that Jesus did! Besides, what makes heaven so amazing is in knowing we deserve to go to hell and through Jesus Christ we can not only be saved from that place, but then He throws heaven in on top? That's what's so amazing! So how does "Do you want to go to heaven" help people get to heaven? Answer? If it's absent of hell, it's not! It's hampering the Gospel, not helping it!

The **3rd phrase** people come up with to try to soften hell is, "Hey man, **you need to get saved."**

Okay, saved from what? A bad life? A mediocre existence? A chicken dinner? A zit, a pimple? What? Saved from what? Don't assume people know what you're talking about because chances are they don't! This is their problem. You need to spell it out for them and say, "You need to get saved from hell!" I didn't say that. Jesus did!

The **4th phrase** people come up with to try to soften hell is, "Hey man, **I don't want to scare them off** with all this hell talk stuff."

Excuse me? Where are you going to scare them off to? Hell #2? What's the option? There is no option. You're either going straight to heaven or you're going straight to hell. But don't listen to me. Listen to these non-Christians who learned the hard way:

- Thomas Payne: "I would give worlds, if I had them, if the Age of Reason had never been published. O Lord, help me! Christ, help me! Stay with me! It is hell to be left alone!"
- Francois Voltaire: "I am abandoned by God and man! I shall go to hell! O' Jesus Christ!"
- David Hume: The atheist died in utter despair with an awful scene crying out, "I am in the flames!"
- Friedrich Nietzsche: Died insane, completely out of his mind.
- Karl Marx: Was on his deathbed surrounded by candles burning to Lucifer and screamed at his nurse who asked him if he had any last words, "Go on, get out! Last words are for fools who haven't said enough."
- J.H. Huxley: The famous agnostic, suddenly looked up and whispered, "So it is true."
- Sir Thomas Scott: "Until now I thought there was no God or hell. Now I know there is both, and I am doomed."
- Sir Francis Newport: "Do not tell me there is no God for I know there is one, and that I am in his angry presence! You need not tell me there is no hell, for I already feel my soul slipping into its fires! I know that I am lost forever."

This is not a game. When in the world are we in the Church going to wake up and deal with reality. There really is a heaven and there really is a hell. And since when did it become unloving to warn somebody from going to a place like that? Rather I'd say you really don't love that person if you refuse to tell them both sides of the story. Why? Because if you really love somebody, you'll love them enough to tell them the truth. I mean, isn't that what Jesus did? In fact, if you think about it, isn't that what makes the birth of Christ, i.e. Christmas, so special? You don't just get your sins forgiven. You get to escape having to go to hell? And that's why I ask you, "Are you ready for the journey?

There really is a heaven and there really is a hell. Scoff all you want, but one day you're going to die and there's nothing you can do to stop it. And if there is one thing that you do not want to get wrong, it is where you will spend eternity. Our last breath here is our first breath in either heaven or hell, and we're going to be dead a lot longer then we are alive. And so, the question you must ask yourself is, "Are you ready for the journey? Have you made adequate preparations? Are you sure that if you were to die today, that you'd go to heaven and not hell?" Well, if you're reading this and you're not sure, then don't delay. Once you're gone, you're not coming back and there is no second chance. Please, I encourage you today, give your life to Jesus *now*, while He may still be found. God loves you and has made a wonderful provision for you to spend eternal bliss with Him in heaven. But you must make that eternal decision that *will* decide your ultimate destiny. Please, give your heart to Jesus. Reach out and accept His love and forgiveness of your sins before its too late. Don't leave this earth without Him. Why? Because *One Second After You Die,* it's going to be too late!

Chapter Four

Is There Really A Heaven?

How many of you out there are one of those people who always has to get the last word in, you know what I'm saying? Well hey, that's right, believe it or not, I've got some good news for you. You see, apparently, you can not only get the last word in here on earth, but apparently, you can now get it in even *after* you leave the earth. How? By doing what these people did with their tombstones. Let's check it out.

- In a Ribbesford, England cemetery appears this message from Anna Wallace, "The children of Israel wanted bread, And the Lord sent them manna, Old clerk Wallace wanted a wife, And the devil sent him Anna."

- Margaret Daniels grave in Richmond, Virginia says, "She always said her feet were killing her, but nobody believed her."
  Anna Hopewell's grave in Enosburg Falls, Vermont says, "Here lies the body of our Anna, done to death by a banana, It wasn't the fruit that laid her low, But the skin of the thing that made her go."

- Harry Edsel Smith's tombstone of Albany, New York says, "Born 1903 – Died 1942. Looked up the elevator shaft to see if the car was on the way down. It was."

- In a Georgia cemetery simply appears this message, "I told you I was sick!"

- Then in an Indiana cemetery is this message, "Pause Stranger, when you pass me by, as you are now, so once was I. As I am now, so you will be, so prepare for death and follow me." An unknown passerby read those words and underneath it scratched this reply, "To follow you I'm not content, Until I know which way you went."

Now how many of you would say that's some good advice? And the purpose of sharing those tombstones with you wasn't merely just to encourage us to get the last word in here on earth, as tempting as that was. But it was actually to encourage us that you better get right with God *before* you leave this earth. Why? Because stepping out into eternity without insurance with God is probably one of the dumbest things you could ever do. I mean, what good is a college tuition or life insurance policy at that point, right? So, here's the point. Don't be like that! Don't make the biggest mistake of your life! Get the proper insurance policy before you leave this earth! His name is Jesus! Accept Him now as your Lord and Savior! Why? Because the Bible says this is not a game! When you die, you're either going straight to heaven or you're going straight to hell! And Jesus is the *only way* to escape the latter!

The **4th objection** that skeptics come up with is this: If there really is life after death, and we're really going to one of two places when we die, and one of those two places really is hell, then **"Is the Other Place Really Heaven?"**

Once again, this is a logical, great straightforward question. I mean, stop and think about it. If all this Jesus stuff is true, and there really is life after death, and we're really going to go to one of two places when we die, and one of those places really is a literal hell, then is the other place really a literal Heaven? Is there really a wonderful alternative to eternal torment and suffering? Of course! God's not just a God of justice. He's a God of love as well! And the Bible is clear. The place He's prepared for those who have received His love and forgiveness through Jesus Christ is not just real, it's really beyond their wildest dreams! But don't take my word for it. Let's listen to God's.

Revelation 21:1-4 "Then I saw a new heaven and a new earth, for the first heaven and the first earth had passed away, and there was no longer any sea. I saw the Holy City, the new Jerusalem, coming down out of heaven from God, prepared as a bride beautifully dressed for her husband. And I heard a loud voice from the throne saying, Now the dwelling of God is with men, and He will live with them. They will be His people, and God Himself will be with them and be their God. He will wipe every tear from their eyes. There will be no more death or mourning or crying or pain, for the old order of things has passed away."

Now according to our text, the Bible clearly says that a place of eternal joy and bliss really does exist, right? I'm not making it up. What did it say there? We're going to be with God Himself in a place beyond our wildest dreams, right? All this dumb, stupid stuff we go through here on earth is gone forever! But that's just the tip of the iceberg. The Bible tells us over and over how wonderful this place is.

- The Dwelling Place of God: (Psalm 2)
- The Dwelling Place of Angels: (Matt. 18)
- A Heavenly Country: (Heb. 11)
- A Holy Place: (Isaiah 57)
- An Eternal Paradise: (1 Cor. 12)

- A Place with Streets of Gold: (Rev. 21)
- A Place with Gates of Pearls: (Rev. 21)
- A Place with Foundations of Precious Gems: (Rev. 21)

- A Place of Eternal Rest: (Rev. 14)
- A Place of Eternal Joy: (Rev. 7)
- A Place Without Wickedness: (Rev. 22)
- A Place Without Darkness: (Rev. 21)
- A Place Without Sin: (Rev. 21)
- A Place Without Tears: (Rev. 21)
- A Place Without Mourning: (Rev. 21)
- A Place Without Pain: (Rev. 21)
- A Place Without Death: (Rev. 21)
- A Place of Absolute Purity: (Rev. 21)
- A Place Filled with the Glory of God: (Rev. 21)
- An Everlasting Place: (2 Cor. 5)

Now maybe it's just me, but I'm kind of thinking, that heaven is one place you really don't want to miss, you know what I'm saying? Therefore, *here's the point*. Who in their right mind would reject God's loving gracious offer to go to a place like that *for free*, especially knowing you deserve to go to the other place and be tormented for eternity? Therefore, to hopefully encourage people to respond to God's loving call to go to heaven before it's too late, we're going to look at three amazing aspects of what happens when we do choose to go to heaven.

The **1st amazing aspect** of going to heaven is **We Get a New Heavenly Body**.

1 Corinthians 15:42,44 "It is the same way for the resurrection of the dead. Our earthly bodies, which die and decay, will be different when they are resurrected, for they will never die. They are natural human bodies now, but when they are raised, they will be spiritual bodies. For just as there are natural bodies, so also there are spiritual bodies."

Now according to out text, the Bible is clear. As you can see, we *will not* continue to exist in heaven as we do now, right? What did it say there? It said we must *out of necessity* be changed in order to partake of our new surroundings, right? And what was the first change mentioned? We're going to get a new *heavenly body*, right? What did it say there? Our bodies will become *imperishable.* Simply put, they will never die, they will never rot, they will never decay, they will never break down, they won't even age. Is that incredible, or what? And think of it. That means, there will be no more back aches, no more broken bones, no more disease, and yes ladies, no more anti-aging creams, to the joy of many, like this lady learned.

"One day there was a four-year-old little girl and she walked into the bathroom while her mother was putting on make-up.

And the little girl announced, 'I'm going to look just like you mommy!' And the mother told her, 'Well yeah, maybe, when you grow up.' And the little girl said, 'No mommy, tomorrow, because I just put on that 'Oil of Old Lady' you always use.'"

Yes ladies, that's right, in heaven there's not going to be anymore "Oil of Old Lady" creams for you to use. Why? Because our bodies will cease to wear down. Which means, there's going to be no more wrinkles, no more crinkles, no more age spots, nothing! None of that stuff. Max Factor will be bankrupt. And we will never have this kind of conversation with our friends again!

"One day a group of Florida senior citizens were sitting around talking about their ailments when one person said, 'My arms are so weak I can hardly hold this cup of coffee.'

'Yes, I know' replied another. 'My cataracts are so bad I can't even see my coffee.'

Then the person with the loudest voice of the group piped in, 'Oh yeah, well it's gotten to where I cannot hear anything anymore.'

Then a fourth person nodded weakly in agreement, 'I know what you mean, I can't turn my head because of the arthritis in my neck.'

'Well, that's nothing,' claimed another 'my blood pressure pills make me dizzy.'

'You think that's bad," said another person, 'Why I can't even remember what I'm doing half the time. If I don't make myself a note I forget what I am trying to do in the first place.'

Then an old wise man of the group winced and shook his head saying, 'I guess that's the price we pay for getting old.'

Then there was a short moment of silence and one woman cheerfully announced, 'Well, it's not that bad. Thank goodness we can all still drive.'"

Wow! Please repeat after me...GET OFF THE ROAD! Anybody glad that in heaven you won't have to deal with that reality or conversation anymore? Why? Because the Bible says our bodies will be *imperishable*! No more will you wake up and go to the breakfast table and you hear snap, crackle, pop, and you discover you're not eating cereal. No more will you go to bed realizing that you and your teeth don't sleep together anymore. No more will you wake up looking like your driver's license picture. And no more will you look for your glasses for half an hour before you realize they were on your head the whole time. You won't need to remember them because you're not going to need them! No more glasses! Our bodies in heaven are going to be *perfect*!

But that's still not all. As if that wasn't cool enough, what else did it say? Our bodies will not only be imperishable, but they'll be what? Spiritual, right? Which means, *our body is going to be like Jesus' body* after He was raised from the dead. And if you study the characteristics of Jesus' resurrected body you're going to see He was *not affected by matter*. I.E. He could walk through doors. He *could travel instantly anywhere*. And yes, for those of you who were wondering, we will still have the ability to eat food. Why? Because the Bible says Jesus ate food with the disciples after His resurrection. Is that great news or what? But I'm telling you, that's still just the tip of the iceberg.

The **2nd amazing aspect** of going to heaven is that **We Get a New Heavenly Abode**.

1 Corinthians 2:9 "That is what the Scriptures mean when they say, 'No eye has seen, no ear has heard, and no mind has imagined what God has prepared for those who love Him.'"

Now according to our text, the Bible clearly says that our new heavenly abode is not only going to be a place prepared for us by God Himself, but it's going to be what? It's going to be absolutely literally unimaginable, right? It's going to be a place beyond our wildest dreams! Why? Because God Himself is making it! Do you expect anything less? In fact, just like the text says, since it's so hard for our minds to conceive how wonderful heaven's going to be, let's try to expand our imagination by taking a look at what this text might mean from a scientific point of view, like this man shares.

"The electromagnetic spectrum contains all the different wavelengths, like radio waves, microwaves, and including a small piece called light. Now your eyeball can see the colors; red, orange, yellow, green, blue, and violet, that's all.

The spectrum goes forever in both directions beyond that. Suppose we get to heaven and God gives us new eyes that can see the entire spectrum. That means there may be brand new colors. Not new shades of our current colors...but brand-new colors!

That's why heaven has to be so large. It's for the women's closets!

But can you imagine if we get new eyes that can see the whole spectrum? You're going to be able to see the sounds coming off the piano. Right now, we can only hear them. Imagine seeing the sounds.

What if we get new ears that can hear the whole spectrum? You're going to be able to hear the colors, or smell them, or taste them!

We've only got five senses folks. Maybe there's more. But if God just took these five and expanded them to the max, we would spend forever walking around heaven going, "Wow! Did you smell that? Here, taste that! Wow!"[1]

Now I don't know about you, but when you look at it scientifically, music coming from flowers is not just possible, but it sounds like that's just the beginning. I don't know about you, but I can't wait to get there! No wonder the Bible says, "No eye has seen, no ear has heard, and no mind has imagined what God has prepared for those who love Him." And I truly believe if we get this, and truly take God at His Word, and focus on this and not this junk on earth, it'll save us a whole lot of heartache here on earth, before we get to heaven, like this guy learned!

"There once was a rich man who was near death and he was very grieved because he'd worked so hard for his money and he wanted to be able to take it with him to heaven. So, he began to pray that he might be able to take some of his wealth with him.

Well, an angel heard his plea and appears to him and say, 'Sorry, but you can't take your wealth with you.' And the man implores the angel to speak to God to see if He might bend the rules a little.

So, the angel goes to God and then reappears and informs the man that God has decided to allow him to take one suitcase with him, that's it! And so overjoyed, the man gathers his largest suitcase and fills it with pure gold bars and places it beside his bed.

And soon afterward the man dies and shows up at the Gates of Heaven to greet St. Peter. And so, St. Peter seeing the suitcase says, 'Hold on, wait a second, you can't bring that in here!'

But, the man explains to St. Peter that he has permission and asks him to verify his story with the Lord. So sure enough, St. Peter checks and comes back saying, 'You're right. You are allowed one carry-on bag, but I'm supposed to check its contents before letting it through.'

And so, St. Peter opens the suitcase to inspect and he exclaims, 'You brought pavement?!!!'"[2]

You brought pavement…how slick the enemy is that he's got us running our lives ragged killing ourselves and each other over pavement. We're headed to a place where the streets are made of gold. And I'd say being reminded of this, our New Heavenly Abode, will save us a whole lot of trouble here on earth, how about you?

The **3rd amazing aspect** of going to heaven is that **We Get a New Heavenly Goodbye**.

1 Corinthians 15:54-55,57-58 "When the perishable has been clothed with the imperishable, and the mortal with immortality, then the saying that is written will come true: Death has been swallowed up in victory. Where, O death, is your victory? Where, O death, is your sting? But thanks be to God! He gives us the victory through our Lord Jesus Christ. Therefore, my dear brothers, stand firm. Let nothing move you."

Now according to our text, when it comes to our time to die as a Christian, we don't have to freak out, we don't have to worry, and we don't even have to be afraid, right? Why? Because what did it say there? We've got the victory through our Lord Jesus Christ. That's why we can stand firm! That's why nothing has to move us. And that's why we can look death square in the face and laugh, ha, ha, ha! You're the loser not me! Why? Because *we know that our last breath here is our first breath in heaven*! In fact, sometimes God gives us a taste of heaven before we even get there, like these guys.

The famous Christian, **Dwight Moody** awoke from sleep shortly before he died and said: "Earth recedes. Heaven opens before me. If this is death, it is sweet! There is no valley here. God is calling me, and I must go." Moody's son said, "No, no, Father. You're dreaming." And Moody replied, "I am not dreaming. I have been within the gates. This is my triumph; this is my coronation day! It is glorious!"

Augustus Toplady, preacher and author of the hymn, "Rock of Ages": "The consolations of God to such an unworthy wretch are so abundant that He leaves me nothing to pray for but a continuance of them. I enjoy heaven already in my soul."

Lady Glenorchy: "If this is dying, it is the pleasantest thing imaginable."

John Pawson, minister: "I know I am dying, but my deathbed is a bed of roses. I have no thorns planted upon my dying pillow. In Christ, heaven is already begun!"

Adoniram Judson, American missionary to Burma: "I go with the gladness of a boy bounding away from school. I feel so strong in Christ."

John A. Lyth: "Can this be death? Why, it is better than living! Tell them I die happy in Jesus!"

Martha McCrackin: "How bright the room! How full of angels!"

Mary Frances: "Oh, that I could tell you what joy I possess! The Lord does shine with such power upon my soul!"

Sir David Brewster, scientist and inventor of the kaleidoscope: "I will see Jesus; I shall see Him as He is! I have had the light for many years. Oh, how bright it is! I feel so safe and satisfied!"

A **Muslim woman**, whose child had died at 16 years of age, asked a Christian missionary, "What did you do to our daughter?" The missionary replied, "We did nothing," But the mother persisted, "Oh, yes, you did! She died smiling. Our people do not die like that." As it turned out, the girl had found Christ and believed on Him only a few months before. Fear of death had gone, and hope and joy had taken its place.

And finally, a **Chinese communist**, through whom many Christians had been executed, said to a Pastor: "I have seen many of you die. The Christians die in a different way. What is your secret?"

I'll tell you what the secret is. It's simply that we Christians have taken God at His Word and we've entrusted our lives to Jesus Christ, and because of this, even our death is now just a pleasant goodbye. And so, I ask you, *one last time*. Is Jesus Christ your Lord and Savior? Have you taken God at His Word that says if you call upon His Name and ask Him to forgive you of all your sins through Jesus Christ, that you'd not go to hell, but instead you'd go to heaven? People, you can scoff all you want, but one day you're going to die and there's nothing you can do to stop it. And so, I beg you, please give your life to Jesus now because *One Second After You Die,* it's going to be too late. Once we're gone, there is no second chance and there is no coming back, and no matter what we try to do to, we will not be successful in delaying the inevitable, like this little girl found out.

"A woman became very ill. After a time of hospitalization, she returned home, but was confined to bed. Her eight-year-old daughter was not aware of the terminal status of the illness.

This little girl stood outside the bedroom door one afternoon as the doctor, along with her father, visited her mother. She overheard the doctor say, 'Yes, I will be frank with you. The time is not too far off. Before the last leaves have gone from the trees you will die.' The little girl's presence was not detected.

Sometime later the father came to the breakfast table to find that his little girl was not there as he had expected. After searching for her he saw her out in the front yard. His heart was broken as he watched her picking up leaves that had begun to fall. She was using thread to tie them back onto the limbs of the tree."

Did you know that we are going to be in eternity a lot longer than we are in this life? And there's absolutely *nothing* we can do to change this reality. Each one of us here is going to make that journey, some sooner than others. So, ask yourself, "Are you sure that if you were to die today, that you'd go to heaven and not hell?" Well, if you're reading this and you're not sure, then

don't delay. Please, I encourage you today, deal with reality, don't deny it. **There Really Is a Heaven** and you **really want to be there**! Remember, God loves you and has made a wonderful provision for you to spend eternal bliss with Him in heaven. But you must make that eternal decision that *will* decide your ultimate destiny. Please, give your heart to Jesus now. Reach out and accept His love and forgiveness of your sins before its too late. Don't leave this earth without Him. Please, go to heaven, don't go to hell! *One Second After You Die*, it's going to be too late!

How to Receive Jesus Christ:

1. Admit your need (I am a sinner).

2. Be willing to turn from your sins (repent).

3. Believe that Jesus Christ died for you on the Cross and rose from the grave.

4. Through prayer, invite Jesus Christ to come in and control your life through the Holy Spirit. (Receive Him as Lord and Savior.)

What to pray:

Dear Lord Jesus,

I know that I am a sinner and need Your forgiveness. I believe that You died for my sins. I want to turn from my sins. I now invite You to come into my heart and life. I want to trust and follow You as Lord and Savior.

In Jesus' name. Amen.

Notes

Chapter 1   *Is There Life After Death?*

1. *Illiteracy*
   https://www.christianretailing.com/index.php/newsletter/the-church-bookstore/180-dec-23-2009/20567-church-life-biblical-illiteracy
2. *George Ritchie*
   https://www.near-death.com/experiences/notable/george-ritchie.html
3. *Howard Storm*
   https://www.near-death.com/experiences/notable/howard-storm.html
4. *Kristine*
   Email story – Source unknown
5. *Bud*
   Email story – Source Unknown
6. *Erwin Lutzer*
   https://verticallivingministries.com/2012/07/18/dr-erwin-lutzer-on-one-of-the-biggest-lies-moderns-believe-about-god/

Chapter 2   *What Happens When You Die?*

1. *A Man called Peter*
   https://www.yidio.com/movie/a-man-called-peter/41359?utm_source=Bing&utm_medium=search&t_source=64&utm_campaign=772&msclkid=c82954c5e434191571080fc01f45aabc
2. *Pastor NDE*
   http://insider.foxnews.com/2015/09/09/90-minutes-heaven-movie-tells-story-don-piper-pastor-pronounced-dead-crash

Chapter 3   *Is There Really a Hell?*

1. *Hell*
   Email Story - Source Unknown
2. *Mal Couch*
   Email Story – Source Unknown

Chapter 4   *Is There Really a Heaven?*

1. *Perfect Body*
   Email Story – Source Unknown
2. *Rich Man*
   Email Story – Source Unknown

Chapter One
Is There Life After Death?

Study

1). The Bible tells us we're either headed for eternal bliss in heaven or what?

2). What percentage of unchurched adults in the US call themselves Christians?

3). Of unchurched adults, 68% believe Satan is only a symbol of evil and doesn't really exist. However, _____% believe that angels exist and influence people's lives.

4). What did Pope Francis tell atheists regarding heaven?

5). What percentage of people who profess to be Christians think Satan is only a symbol of evil and doesn't really exist?

6). What percentage of professing Christians believe they will NOT go to heaven?

7). Why don't NDE's (Near Death Experiences) give us a definitive answer on whether or not there is life after death?

8). What chapter and verse in the book of Daniel give us the definitive answer on whether or not there is life after death?

9). Psalm 9:17 and Psalm 30:3 give two examples of people who went to Sheol, the _____ and the _____.

10). In Luke chapter 16, Jesus tells the story of the rich man and Lazarus. What is separating them in Sheol?

11). What happened to the righteous saints in Sheol once Jesus was resurrected from the dead?

12). Since the Resurrection, where do believers go now when they die?

13). When an unbeliever dies, where do they go, and is their permanent location?

14). According to Luke 16, is it possible to have communication with the dead?

15). If a person does hear a voice or see an apparition, it is not your Aunt Vera, what is it?

16). What does Deuteronomy 18 tell us God does not permit us to do?

17). Revelation 20:11-15 tells us the final destination for the unrighteous. What is it and when does it occur?

Chapter Two
What Happens When You Die?

Study

1). Romans chapter 1 says men claim to be wise but are in fact what?

2). God made His existence known through the _____ of His creation.

3). How many times could you fill the Grand Canyon if you typed out our DNA code into books?

4). What does evolution say happens when we die?

5). What does the Bible say happens when we die?

6). The theory of "Little gods" is a logical absurdity. Explain why.

7). What is the theory of reincarnation?

8). What type of birth is John 3:3 referring to?

9). God says we live only once, die once, and then what happens?

10). Pastor Billy gives us two scriptures that prove we do not enter "soul sleep" upon death. What are they?

11). Who were the two people talking with Jesus and the transfiguration in Matthew 17 who were very much alive and not taking a nap?

12). What is the false Catholic teaching that says we go to some "holding pen" to purge our sins after death?

13). What makes this a blasphemous doctrine?

14). How many of our sins were covered by Jesus' death on the cross?

15). Name the five ways the Bible likens death for the Christian.

Chapter Three
Is There Really a Hell?

Study

1). What are the statistics on death?

2). What did Jesus teach about more than anything else?

3). What was the Valley of Hinnom used for in the time of Jesus?

4). Pastor Billy gives us 20 descriptions of hell from the Bible. Name five of them and the scripture reference.

5). What is Universalism?

6). How long does hell last according to Matthew 25:46?

7). What is annihilationism?

8). If annihilation were true, would it be a punishment or a release from punishment?

9). What must we do to cease being a child of the devil and become a child of God?

10). God must punish wickedness because he is _____.

11). God didn't have to, but he provided a way out of hell. What was it?

12). How does the phrase "Christless Eternity" help the lost realize that they're going to hell unless they get right with God?

13). What does Pastor Billy say is so amazing about heaven?

14). What do people need to get saved from?

15). Is it loving not to tell someone about hell?

Chapter Four
Is There Really a Heaven?

Study

1). What is the proper insurance policy you need before leaving this earth?

2). Pastor Billy gives us 20 attributes of Heaven. Name five of them and the scripture references.

3). According to 1 Corinthians 15:42,44, what kind of body will we have in heaven?

4). Name something Jesus did in his resurrected body that we cannot do in our current physical bodies.

5). Pastor Billy tells the joke of the old man bringing something with him to heaven. In reality, what was it that he brought?

6). Who is the one that is preparing a place for us?

7). Why as a Christian do we not have to be afraid of death?

Made in the USA
Middletown, DE
24 February 2019